BRIGHTER CHILD

Handwriting: Printing

Grades K-2

P9-DCQ-746

CARSON-DELLOSA™
PUBLISHING GROUP

Greensboro, NC 27425 USA

Brighter Child®
An imprint of Carson-Dellosa Publishing LLC
P.O. Box 35665
Greensboro, NC 27425 USA

Printed in the USA • All rights reserved.   ISBN 978-1-4838-1642-5

01-062157784

Name _____

Practice by tracing the letter. Then write the letter.

Handwriting: Printing

A B C D E F G H I J K L M N O P Q R S T U V W X Y Z

Practice by tracing the letter. Then write the letter.

B   B   B   B   B   B   B

b   b   b   b   b   b   b

A B **C** D E F G H I J K L M N O P Q R S T U V W X Y Z

Practice by tracing the letter. Then write the letter.

C C C C C C C

c c c c c c c

Handwriting: Printing

A B C **D** E F G H I J K L M N O P Q R S T U V W X Y Z

Practice by tracing the letter. Then write the letter.

| A | B | C | D | E | F | G | H | I | J | K | L | M | N | O | P | Q | R | S | T | U | V | W | X | Y | Z |

Practice by tracing the letter. Then write the letter.

Handwriting: Printing

A B C D E F G H I J K L M N O P Q R S T U V W X Y Z

Practice by tracing the letter. Then write the letter.

Name _____

Practice by tracing the letter. Then write the letter.

G G G G G G G G

g g g g g g g

Handwriting: Printing

A B C D E F G **H** I J K L M N O P Q R S T U V W X Y Z

Practice by tracing the letter. Then write the letter.

A B C D E F G H I J K L M N O P Q R S T U V W X Y Z

Practice by tracing the letter. Then write the letter.

Handwriting: Printing

A B C D E F G H I J K L M N O P Q R S T U V W X Y Z

Practice by tracing the letter. Then write the letter.

| A | B | C | D | E | F | G | H | I | J | **K** | L | M | N | O | P | Q | R | S | T | U | V | W | X | Y | Z |

Practice by tracing the letter. Then write the letter.

K   K   K   K   K   K   K   K

K   K   K   K   K   K   K

A B C D E F G H I J K L M N O P Q R S T U V W X Y Z

Practice by tracing the letter. Then write the letter.

A B C D E F G H I J K L **M** N O P Q R S T U V W X Y Z

Practice by tracing the letter. Then write the letter.

M M M M M M M M

m m m m m m m m

Handwriting: Printing

A B C D E F G H I J K L M **N** O P Q R S T U V W X Y Z

Practice by tracing the letter. Then write the letter.

N N N N N N N

n n n n n n n

A B C D E F G H I J K L M N O P Q R S T U V W X Y Z

Practice by tracing the letter. Then write the letter.

Handwriting: Printing

| A | B | C | D | E | F | G | H | I | J | K | L | M | N | O | **P** | Q | R | S | T | U | V | W | X | Y | Z |

Practice by tracing the letter. Then write the letter.

P P P P P P P P

p p p p p p p

A B C D E F G H I J K L M N O P Q R S T U V W X Y Z

Practice by tracing the letter. Then write the letter.

Q   Q   Q   Q   Q   Q   Q

a   a   a   a   a   a   a

Handwriting: Printing

A B C D E F G H I J K L M N O P Q R S T U V W X Y Z

Practice by tracing the letter. Then write the letter.

R   R   R   R   R   R   R   R

r   r   r   r   r   r   r   r

Name _____

Practice by tracing the letter. Then write the letter.

S   S   S   S   S   S   S

S   S   S   S   S   S   S

Handwriting: Printing

A B C D E F G H I J K L M N O P Q R S T U V W X Y Z

Practice by tracing the letter. Then write the letter.

Handwriting: Printing

© Carson-Dellosa

A B C D E F G H I J K L M N O P Q R S T **U** V W X Y Z

Practice by tracing the letter. Then write the letter.

Handwriting: Printing

| A | B | C | D | E | F | G | H | I | J | K | L | M | N | O | P | Q | R | S | T | U | **V** | W | X | Y | Z |

Practice by tracing the letter. Then write the letter.

Name _____

Practice by tracing the letter. Then write the letter.

W W W W W W W W

W W W W W W W

© Carson-Dellosa

Handwriting: Printing

A B C D E F G H I J K L M N O P Q R S T U V W X Y Z

Practice by tracing the letter. Then write the letter.

Name _____

Practice by tracing the letter. Then write the letter.

Handwriting: Printing

A B C D E F G H I J K L M N O P Q R S T U V W X Y **Z**

Practice by tracing the letter. Then write the letter.

Handwriting: Printing

© Carson-Dellosa

A B C D E F G H I J K L M N O P Q R S T U V W X Y Z

Practice by tracing the words. Then write the words.

alligator

apple

ant

Alaska

Handwriting: Printing

Name _____

Practice by tracing the words. Then write the words.

bear

ball

bee

Bobby

A B C D E F G H I J K L M N O P Q R S T U V W X Y Z

Practice by tracing the words. Then write the words.

cats

cookies

cards

Chuck

Handwriting: Printing

A B C D E F G H I J K L M N O P Q R S T U V W X Y Z

Practice by tracing the words. Then write the words.

duck

dog

dance

Danny

A B C D **E** **F G H I J K L M N O P Q R S T U V W X Y Z**

Practice by tracing the words. Then write the words.

elephant

egg

elbow

Ellie

Handwriting: Printing

A B C D E **F** G H I J K L M N O P Q R S T U V W X Y Z

Practice by tracing the words. Then write the words.

frog

fish

fox

Florida

A B C D E F G H I J K L M N O P Q R S T U V W X Y Z

Practice by tracing the words. Then write the words.

giraffe

grass

glasses

Gretchen

Handwriting: Printing

A B C D E F G H I J K L M N O P Q R S T U V W X Y Z

Practice by tracing the words. Then write the words.

hippo

hat

heart

Hannah

A B C D E F G H **I** J K L M N O P Q R S T U V W X Y Z

Practice by tracing the words. Then write the words.

inchworm

iguana

igloo

Indiana

Handwriting: Printing

A B C D E F G H I J K L M N O P Q R S T U V W X Y Z

Practice by tracing the words. Then write the words.

jaguar

jump

jam

June

A B C D E F G H I J K L M N O P Q R S T U V W X Y Z

Practice by tracing the words. Then write the words.

kangaroo

kite

key

Kelsey

Handwriting: Printing

A B C D E F G H I J K L M N O P Q R S T U V W X Y Z

Practice by tracing the words. Then write the words.

lion

lollipop

lick

Lori

| A | B | C | D | E | F | G | H | I | J | K | L | **M** | N | O | P | Q | R | S | T | U | V | W | X | Y | Z |

Practice by tracing the words. Then write the words.

monkey

mushroom

moon

Megan

Handwriting: Printing

A B C D E F G H I J K L M N O P Q R S T U V W X Y Z

Practice by tracing the words. Then write the words.

newt

nest

note

Nebraska

Handwriting: Printing

© Carson-Dellosa

A B C D E F G H I J K L M N O P Q R S T U V W X Y Z

Practice by tracing the words. Then write the words.

ostrich

octopus

olive

Olivia

Handwriting: Printing

| A | B | C | D | E | F | G | H | I | J | K | L | M | N | O | **P** | Q | R | S | T | U | V | W | X | Y | Z |

Practice by tracing the words. Then write the words.

penguin

pizza

pencil

puppy

A B C D E F G H I J K L M N O P Q R S T U V W X Y Z

Practice by tracing the words. Then write the words.

quail

queen

quarter

quit

Handwriting: Printing

| A | B | C | D | E | F | G | H | I | J | K | L | M | N | O | P | Q | **R** | S | T | U | V | W | X | Y | Z |

Practice by tracing the words. Then write the words.

rabbit

ribbon

race

runs

A B C D E F G H I J K L M N O P Q R S T U V W X Y Z

Practice by tracing the words. Then write the words.

seat

sun

shell

seven

Handwriting: Printing

A B C D E F G H I J K L M N O P Q R S T U V W X Y Z

Practice by tracing the words. Then write the words.

turtle

tiger

tie

teach

Name _____

Practice by tracing the words. Then write the words.

umpire

umbrella

under

unhappy

Handwriting: Printing

A B C D E F G H I J K L M N O P Q R S T U V W X Y Z

Practice by tracing the words. Then write the words.

vulture

violin

vest

van

Name _____

Practice by tracing the words. Then write the words.

whale

walrus

water

wishes

Handwriting: Printing

| A | B | C | D | E | F | G | H | I | J | K | L | M | N | O | P | Q | R | S | T | U | V | W | **X** | Y | Z |

Practice by tracing the words. Then write the words.

X-ray

Xylophone

Max

Extra

A B C D E F G H I J K L M N O P Q R S T U V W X Y Z

Practice by tracing the words. Then write the words.

yak

yo-yo

yarn

Your

Handwriting: Printing

A B C D E F G H I J K L M N O P Q R S T U V W X Y Z

Practice by tracing the words. Then write the words.

zebra

zipper

zoo

zigzag

Name _____

Write the sentence.

Alligators and ants

eat apples.

Handwriting: Printing

A B C D E F G H I J K L M N O P Q R S T U V W X Y Z

Write the sentence.

Brave Bobby buys a
baseball bat.

Handwriting: Printing

© Carson-Dellosa

A B **C** D E F G H I J K L M N O P Q R S T U V W X Y Z

Write the sentence.

Cool cats play cards.

Handwriting: Printing

A B C **D** E F G H I J K L M N O P Q R S T U V W X Y Z

Write the sentence.

Danny dances with a
dandy dog.

Handwriting: Printing   © Carson-Dellosa

A B C D E F G H I J K L M N O P Q R S T U V W X Y Z

Write the sentence.

Every evening Ellie eats

eggs.

Handwriting: Printing

A B C D E **F** G H I J K L M N O P Q R S T U V W X Y Z

Write the sentence.

Four foxes and five fish fly
to Florida.

Name _____

Write the sentence.

Gretchen wears gray glasses.

Handwriting: Printing

A B C D E F G **H** I J K L M N O P Q R S T U V W X Y Z

Write the sentence.

Hannah hears a hungry hippo.

Handwriting: Printing

A B C D E F G H **I** **J K L M N O P Q R S T U V W X Y Z**

Write the sentence.

Inchworms itch in Indiana.

Handwriting: Printing

Name _____

A B C D E F G H I **J** K L M N O P Q R S T U V W X Y Z

Write the sentence.

Jumping jaguars tell jolly jokes.

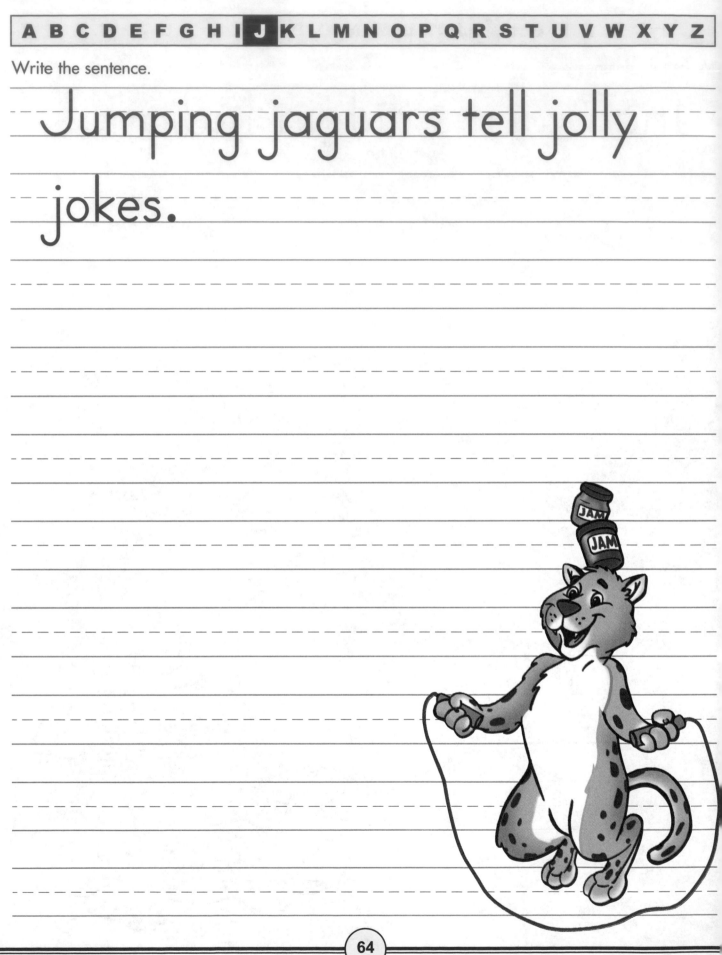

Name _____

Write the sentence.

Kind Kelsey keeps
kangaroos.

Handwriting: Printing

A B C D E F G H I J K **L** M N O P Q R S T U V W X Y Z

Write the sentence.

Little Lori likes lions and
lollipops.

Handwriting: Printing

© Carson-Dellosa

A B C D E F G H I J K L **M** N O P Q R S T U V W X Y Z

Write the sentence.

Mommy monkeys mash
Megan's mushrooms.

Handwriting: Printing

A B C D E F G H I J K L M **N** O P Q R S T U V W X Y Z

Write the sentence.

Nine newts have no nest.

A	B	C	D	E	F	G	H	I	J	K	L	M	N	**O**	P	Q	R	S	T	U	V	W	X	Y	Z

Write the sentence.

Olivia owns one ostrich and

one octopus.

Handwriting: Printing

A B C D E F G H I J K L M N O **P** Q R S T U V W X Y Z

Write the sentence.

The penguin plays in the pretty pool.

Handwriting: Printing

© Carson-Dellosa

Name _____

Write the sentence.

The quiet queen quits quarreling.

Handwriting: Printing

A B C D E F G H I J K L M N O P Q **R** S T U V W X Y Z

Write the sentence.

Rowdy rabbits run a road race.

A B C D E F G H I J K L M N O P Q R **S** T U V W X Y Z

Write the sentence.

Seven shells shine in the soft sunshine.

Handwriting: Printing

A B C D E F G H I J K L M N O P Q R S **T** U V W X Y Z

Write the sentence.

Ten turtles teach tigers.

Handwriting: Printing

© Carson-Dellosa

Name _____

Write the sentence.

Unhappy umpires use ugly umbrellas.

Handwriting: Printing

Name _____

Write the sentence.

Vultures in vests play violins.

Handwriting: Printing

© Carson-Dellosa

A B C D E F G H I J K L M N O P Q R S T U V W X Y Z

Write the sentence.

A walrus wishes for warm

water.

Handwriting: Printing

A B C D E F G H I J K L M N O P Q R S T U V W X Y Z

Write the sentence.

Max got extra xylophones
and saxophones.

© Carson-Dellosa

Name _____

Write the sentence.

Your yak plays with a
yellow yo-yo.

© Carson-Dellosa

Handwriting: Printing

A B C D E F G H I J K L M N O P Q R S T U V W X Y Z

Write the sentence.

Zany zebras zigzag through the zoo.